Living in a World of
blue
Where Survival Means Blending In

Tanya Lee Stone

BLACKBIRCH PRESS, INC.
WOODBRIDGE, CONNECTICUT

For my husband Alan, my true blue love.

Published by Blackbirch Press, Inc.
260 Amity Road
Woodbridge, CT 06525

Email: staff@blackbirch.com
Web site: www.blackbirch.com

©2001 by Blackbirch Press, Inc.
First Edition

Printed in the United States

10 9 8 7 6 5 4 3 2 1

Photo Credits: All images ©Corel Corporation, except pages 3, 17: ©PhotoDisc, Inc.; page 7: © www.arttoday.com.

Library of Congress Cataloging-in-Publication Data
Stone, Tanya Lee.
Living in a world of blue / by Tanya Lee Stone.
    p.   cm.
ISBN 1-56711-581-0 (hardcover: alk. paper)
1. Marine animals —Juvenile literature. [1. Marine Animals. 2. Animals — Habits and behavior. 3. Adaptation (Biology)] I. Title.
QL122.S795 2001
578.77—dc21   2001002365

Contents

What do all the animals in this book have in common?
They all live in a world of blue. They make their homes in the Earth's
oceans and seas. These 10 animals are perfectly suited to their watery world.
They can breathe underwater with gills. And most have fins that they use
for swimming. Each one of these creatures also has special ways to hunt
food and to find protection from danger. How do they do it?

Lizard Fishes

Sneaky Snatchers

There are many different kinds of lizard fishes. Most live in shallow waters. A lizard fish buries itself in the sandy bottom for camouflage. Camouflage means that it blends into its background. A lizard fish also has splotchy markings that help it blend in. Sometimes only the head and eyes of a lizard fish can be seen sticking up out of the sand. It can sit this way for hours. A lizard fish hides to avoid danger and spring a surprise attack on its next meal.

Did You Know?

Some decorator crabs stop "dressing up" when they grow too big to have many predators.

Masking Crabs
Devious Decorators

Masking crabs and decorator crabs can fool their enemies while they hide right out in the open water. They can also surprise their prey. These crabs use strong pincer claws to place all kinds of living things on their backs. They use seaweed, sea sponges, and anemones. They also use algae, coral, and other bits of sea life to "decorate" themselves. This camouflage material sticks to the crab's shell and legs with the help of its tiny hook-shaped hairs. The crab is often so well disguised that it can't be seen unless it moves.

Decorator crabs pull many kinds of ocean materials onto their backs for camouflage.

Did You Know?

One kind of stonefish has the deadliest venom of all fishes. The poison is so powerful that an adult human could die from a stonefish sting.

Stonefish
Bumps that Blend

Like the lizard fish, a stonefish also hides on shallow bottoms. The stonefish, however, hides in a rocky area instead of a sandy one. Tide pools and coral reefs are perfect habitats for this bumpy, rocky shaped fish. Blending in makes it easy for a stonefish to catch its prey. Small crabs and fish think they're swimming by a rock—until the rock jumps out and snatches them!

A stonefish's camouflage also helps it stay hidden from danger. But that's not its only weapon. A stonefish has sharp spines on its back. These spines are filled with venom (poison). If it senses danger, a stonefish will shoot the venom out of its spines.

9

<u>Did You Know?</u>

- This graceful ray gets its name from the Spanish word manta, which means blanket or cloak.
- A Manta ray's wingspan can be more than 20 feet (6 meters) wide.

Manta Rays
Winged Wonders

Manta rays live in the Atlantic, Pacific, and Indian oceans. They are some of the largest animals in the ocean. These large creatures eat only small fish, shrimp, and plankton (tiny plants and animals that float in the sea). How does such a big animal get enough of this tiny food? It has a huge mouth that can open very wide. On each side of a manta's head are large lobes—similar to human ear lobes. These horn-shaped lobes help funnel food into a manta's wide-open mouth.

Mantas don't have many enemies. Although they are large, they are well camouflaged. Seen from above, their dark tops blend in with the dark water below. Seen from below, their white bellies blend in with the brightness of the water's surface.

Did You Know?

- A peacock flounder is born with an eye on each side of its head. A few months later, the right eye shifts over to the left side!
- Each of a flounder's eyes works independently. This way, it can be on the lookout for food and danger from every direction.

Flounders

Flat Floor-dwellers

There are many types of flounders in the world's oceans. They all have flat bodies. In fact, flounders belong to a group called flatfishes. Flounders spend much of their time hidden on the sea floor. They dig themselves in with their fins and throw sand up onto their bodies. This gives them excellent camouflage protection from predators. A peacock flounder has beautiful blue spots. It can even change the shade of blue to better match its sandy surroundings.

A peacock flounder is one of the "left-eye" flounders. These fish only have eyes on the left side of their head. When a flounder is buried in the sand, only its eyes can be seen.

Did You Know?

- Squid can swim up to 25 miles per hour (40 kilometers per hour).
- Squid use color changes and their own form of sign language to communicate with each other.

Squid
Squishy Swift Swimmers

Squid are relatives of the octopus.
An octopus, however, lives near
the ocean floor. It has many
places to hide. A squid
lives in the open
ocean, where life can
be very dangerous.
Unlike the octopus, a squid
has an almost clear, silvery body. This helps it blend in well in
the open water. It also makes squid hard to see when they swim
near the water's surface.

One of a squid's best defenses is speed. It is one of the
fastest swimmers in the sea. Speed also helps a squid hunt.

Did You Know?

Like its relative the seahorse, a female pipefish places her eggs in the male's pouch. The male then carries its eggs until they hatch.

Pipefish
Long and Lean

The seahorse is a close relative of the pipefish.

A pipefish's name describes it well. It has a long, slim, pipe-shaped body. There are many kinds of pipefish in the world's oceans. Pipefish do not have scales like most fishes. Instead, they are covered with reptile-like plates. The tiny seahorse is a relative of the pipefish.

Some sea creatures, like the squid, use speed to escape danger. But pipefish are not the best swimmers. They must rely on camouflage for protection. Both their color and shape protect them. Some pipefish are shades of green, which match seaweed or kelp. Others have bright colors that blend in with coral. Most pipefish stay in shallow waters. They often hover upright in kelp or seaweed beds. That way, their tall, slender shape is hard to see among the strands of seaweed.

Did You Know?

- Most sharks can sense electrical signals that are created by other living things in the ocean.
- Most sharks will sink in the water if they stop swimming.
- A shark can smell prey more than 650 feet (198 meters) away.

Sharks

Expert Hunters

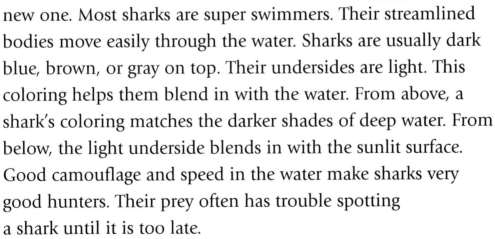

Sharks are among the best predators in the ocean. They have powerful jaws filled with razor-sharp teeth. When a shark loses or breaks a tooth, it grows a new one. Most sharks are super swimmers. Their streamlined bodies move easily through the water. Sharks are usually dark blue, brown, or gray on top. Their undersides are light. This coloring helps them blend in with the water. From above, a shark's coloring matches the darker shades of deep water. From below, the light underside blends in with the sunlit surface. Good camouflage and speed in the water make sharks very good hunters. Their prey often has trouble spotting a shark until it is too late.

Did You Know?

The largest eel in the ocean is the Giant Moray. It can grow up to 10 feet (3.1 meters) long and weigh up to 75 pounds (34 kilograms).

Moray Eels

Reef Ready

There are about 100 different kinds of moray eels. Most live in sheltered places such as coral reefs. Morays come in a wide variety of colors and markings. Their appearance camouflages them well among the colors and shapes of a coral reef. Even the inside of a moray's mouth is camouflaged. They need this extra protection because they spend a lot of time with their mouths open. Although a moray might look hungry with its mouth open wide, it is actually just breathing. It has small gills inside its mouth that filter oxygen from the water.

Morays have very strong, snakelike bodies. They will attack and eat animals as large as an octopus. A moray will tie its muscular body in a knot around an octopus. Then it chomps into the prey with its strong jaws and sharp teeth.

Did You Know?

The Pygmy Goby is the smallest vertebrate (animal with a backbone) on Earth. Most are less than a half-inch (1.2 centimeters) long.

Gobies
Sticking Together

There are more than 1,500 different kinds of goby fish. Many gobies make burrows in the sandy or muddy water bottoms. Some will perch on a rock or ledge near the bottom. With colors and markings that blend with the surroundings, these small fish can go unnoticed by larger predators. Gobies often have large eyes and see very well. They can gobble up small prey as it drifts by.

Some gobies live with shrimp. The two actually help each other to survive. Shrimp cannot see well and have trouble sensing danger. A large-eyed goby is a perfect look-out. It alerts the shrimp to danger so both can escape into the burrow they share.

Glossary

Camouflage Any behavior or appearance that helps disguise an animal in its environment.

Parasite An animal or plant that lives on another in order to get all or part of its food.

Plankton Tiny animals that float in the sea or other body of water.

Predator An animal that hunts other animals for food.

Prey An animal that is hunted by another animal.

Venom A poison produced by some animals.

Vertebrate An animal with a backbone.

For More Information

Books

Seward, H. *Sea Monsters: Eels, Frightening Fish, Manatees, Octopus and Squid, Rays and Sea Snakes.* The Rourke Book Company, 1999.

Taylor, Barbara, Robin Kerrod, Mike Bright. *Nature's Wild Predators: Life and Survival in the Wild.* Chicago, IL: Lorenz Books, 2000.

Web Site

Learn more about ocean creatures at:

http://www.discovery.com/stories/nature/creatures/creatures.html

Index